Witney and Bubba
Lost and Found

Written by Zoë Clarke

Illustrated by Felicia Whaley

Collins

This is Witney.

Witney
Age nine
Likes Boscoe

Job lost and found agent

This is Boscoe.

 **Boscoe**

Age seven

Likes Witney

Job catching, fetching, itching

3

Witney and Boscoe are at Reeva's pie shop.
In the window there are pictures of lost things.

trolley

LOST

cage

Little April

keys

Witney and Boscoe are searching for Little April.

Let's fetch the finding kit!

This is Witney's finding kit.

adventure map

little blanket

long cable

heavy rope

bag for clues

Witney snatched the washing bag by mistake!

Hurry, Boscoe!

7

They found one clue by some giant honey bees.

Little April's bow! We need the bag for clues.

Witney opened the bag.

There was an apron with useful pockets.

As they bustled off, they saw some paw prints

Witney looked in the bag.

There were lots of socks.

Carefully, Witney made a sock rope and tied it to a tall tree.

She grabbed Boscoe and jumped!

They landed in a scratchy bush.

We need the little blanket.

Witney looked in the bag.

There were matching jumpers.

They wrapped the matching jumpers round their heads.

Little April's coat! Fetch it, Boscoe.

16

Boscoe snatched the coat.

There was Little April! April was not little.

We need the heavy rope.

Witney looked in the bag.

There was a tie and some tights.

We need the adventure map to get home.

The bag was empty, but Boscoe found the park map and the trolley!

20

Witney put Boscoe and Little April in the trolley.

Just the keys and cage to find. Maybe next time!

Adventure map

❧ Review: After reading ❧

Use your assessment from hearing the children read to choose any GPCs, words or tricky words that need additional practice.

Read 1: Decoding

- Look through the book together. Ask the children:
  - Can you spot words with the /ch/ sound? (*itching, snatched, ditch, fetching, scratchy, matching, catching*)
  - Can you point to the letters that make the /ch/ sound in each of these words? (*tch*)

Read 2: Prosody

- Choose two double page spreads and model reading with expression to the children.
- Ask the children to have a go at reading the same pages with expression.
- On page 5, show the children how you read the speech bubbles using expression. For the other speech bubbles, discuss with the children how Witney would say these things.

Read 3: Comprehension

- Turn to pages 22 and 23 and ask the children to follow the adventure map with their finger. Can they retell the story in their own words?
- For every question ask the children how they know the answer. Ask:
  - What are Witney and Boscoe looking for? (*Little April*)
  - What bag does Witney take instead of her finding kit? (*the washing bag*)
  - What clues do Witney and Boscoe find? (*a bow, paw prints, a coat*)
  - Can you remember what items Witney found in the washing bag? (*socks, tights, a tie, two matching jumpers and an apron*)